PIANO / VOCAL

Sarah Vaughan
ORIGINAL KEYS FOR SINGERS

Cover Photo: The Frank Driggs Collection

ISBN 0-634-06787-7

**HAL•LEONARD®
CORPORATION**

7777 W. BLUEMOUND RD. P.O. BOX 13819 MILWAUKEE, WI 53213

For all works contained herein:
Unauthorized copying, arranging, adapting, recording or public performance is an infringement of copyright.
Infringers are liable under the law.

Visit Hal Leonard Online at
www.halleonard.com

Sarah Vaughan

Contents

4	BIOGRAPHY
136	DISCOGRAPHY
5	After Hours
10	Black Coffee
16	Body and Soul
21	But Not for Me
26	Cheek to Cheek
35	Cherokee (Indian Love Song)
42	Darn That Dream
48	East of the Sun (And West of the Moon)
58	If You Could See Me Now
62	Isn't This a Lovely Day (To Be Caught in the Rain)
68	It Might as Well Be Spring
74	It Shouldn't Happen to a Dream (How Could It Happen to a Dream)
53	Lullaby of Birdland
80	The Man I Love
85	Misty
90	My Funny Valentine
94	My Ship
98	The Nearness of You
102	A Night in Tunisia
112	An Occasional Man
105	Perdido
116	Send in the Clowns
124	September Song
129	Spring Will Be a Little Late This Year
132	Tenderly

Biography

The Divine One, the one and only Sarah Vaughan, was more than just a jazz singer coming to be in a golden age. She was a pure voice, a sassy entertainer, and one of the finest musicians of her era. While most singers' voices diminish with age, Sarah's expanded in range, allowing her to reach from a mellow baritone note to the highest soprano. Often considered to be in the elite company of great vocalists Ella Fitzgerald and Billie Holiday, Sarah was an innovator throughout her forty-year recording career. While Ella often gained the most universal admiration and Billie was the most iconic, Sarah was the talent, the truly gifted singer.

Born in Newark, New Jersey, on March 27, 1924, Sarah Vaughan grew up surrounded by music. From her countless piano and organ lessons to her love for singing in the Mt. Zion Baptist Church choir, she developed quickly as a talented young woman. At the age of just 19 years old, Sarah won an amateur contest at the Apollo Theatre for her rendition of "Body and Soul," which in turn won her a ticket to join Earl Hines as a singer and pianist in his big band. A year later, she left to join Billy Eckstine's orchestra. It was through this gig that she met a couple of his innovative sidemen: Dizzy Gillespie and Charlie Parker. Her sophisticated understanding and amazing technique allowed her to become a peer among these bebop icons.

By 1946, Sarah Vaughan began recording and performing as a soloist, which inevitably led to her international stardom. From the pioneering bebop recordings with Gillespie and others in the mid 1940s to her memorable classics with Columbia Records through 1954, Vaughan became one of the most beloved singers amongst both fans and jazz musicians. She made great records with labels Mercury and Roulette through the late 1960s.

After a brief hiatus, Sarah returned to recording with a deepened voice, still exhibiting the power and range of her earlier years. Her scatting abilities were nearly unrivaled as she created some unforgettable jazz records for Mainstream from 1971-74 and with Norman Granz's Pablo label from 1977-82. She continued to make great public performances nearly until her death on April 3, 1990.

She was called "Sassy" because of her relentless wit, but was known as the "Divine One" because of her astonishing vocal abilities. Sarah was an idol and influence to other singers, musicians, and enthusiasts as well. There is no doubt that Sarah Vaughan will always be remembered as one of the most remarkable musicians of our time.

AFTER HOURS

Words by ROBERT BRUCE and BUDDY FEYNE
Music by AVERY PARRISH

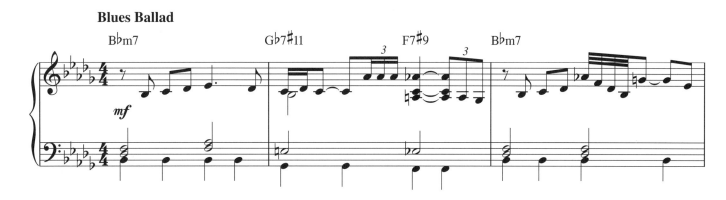
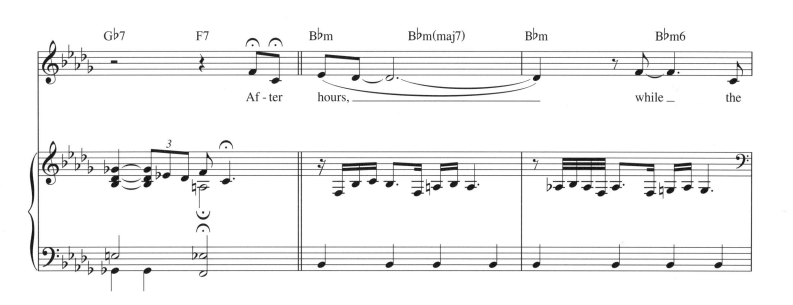

Copyright © 1946 by Popular Music Co.
Copyright Renewed, Assigned to Chappell & Co.
International Copyright Secured   All Rights Reserved

BLACK COFFEE

Words and Music by PAUL FRANCIS WEBSTER
and SONNY BURKE

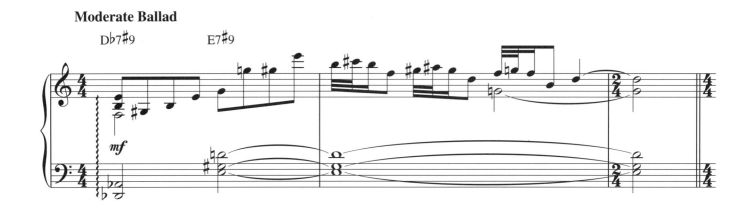

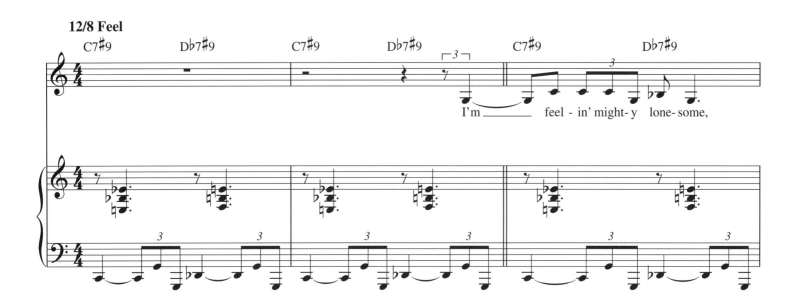

Copyright © 1948 (Renewed) Webster Music Co. and Sondot Music Corporation
International Copyright Secured   All Rights Reserved

BODY AND SOUL

Words by EDWARD HEYMAN,
ROBERT SOUR and FRANK EYTON
Music by JOHN GREEN

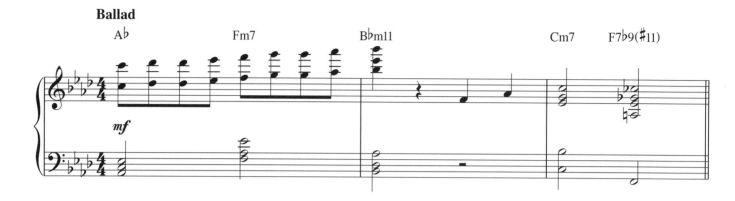

Copyright © 1930 WARNER BROS. INC.
Copyright renewed; extended term of Copyright deriving from Edward Heyman assigned and effective January 1, 1987 to Range Road Music Inc. and Quartet Music, Inc.
Extended term of Copyright deriving from John Green, Robert Sour and Frank Eyton assigned to Warner Bros. Inc. and Druropetal Music
This arrangement Copyright © 1993 Road Music Inc., Quartet Music, Inc., Warner Bros. Inc. and Druropetal Music
International Copyright Secured All Rights Reserved
Used by Permission

20

BUT NOT FOR ME

Music and Lyrics by GEORGE GERSHWIN
and IRA GERSHWIN

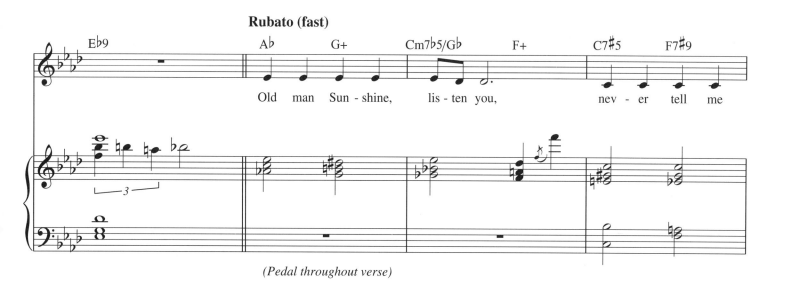

(Pedal throughout verse)

© 1930 WB MUSIC CORP. (Renewed)
All Rights Reserved   Used by Permission

CHEEK TO CHEEK
from the RKO Radio Motion Picture TOP HAT

Words and Music by
IRVING BERLIN

© Copyright 1935 by Irving Berlin
Copyright Renewed
International Copyright Secured   All Rights Reserved

28

CHEROKEE
(Indian Love Song)

Words and Music by
RAY NOBLE

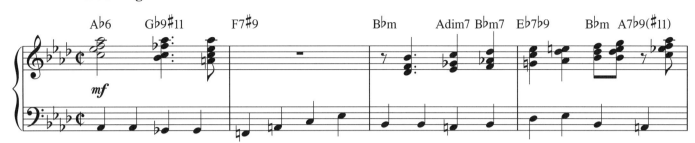

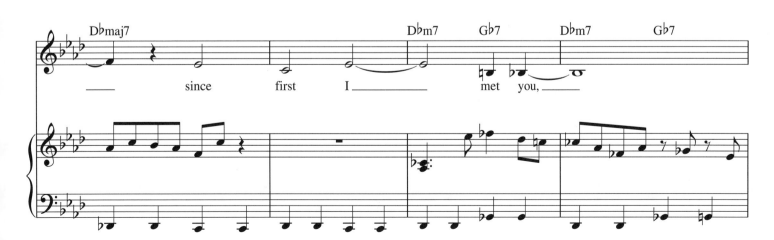

Copyright © 1938 The Peter Maurice Music Co., Ltd., London, England
Copyright Renewed and Assigned to Shapiro, Bernstein & Co., Inc., New York for U.S.A. and Canada
International Copyright Secured   All Rights Reserved
Used by Permission

DARN THAT DREAM

Lyric by EDDIE DE LANGE
Music by JIMMY VAN HEUSEN

Copyright © 1939 WB Music Corp.
Copyright Renewed, Assigned and Copyright © 1968 by Scarsdale Music Corporation and Music Sales Corporation
International Copyright Secured   All Rights Reserved
Used by Permission

EAST OF THE SUN
(And West of the Moon)

Words and Music by
BROOKS BOWMAN

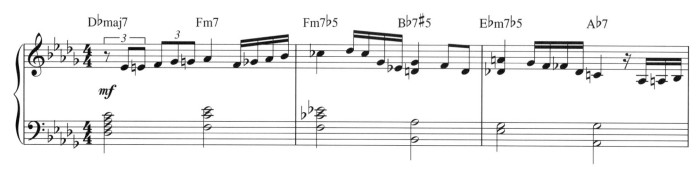
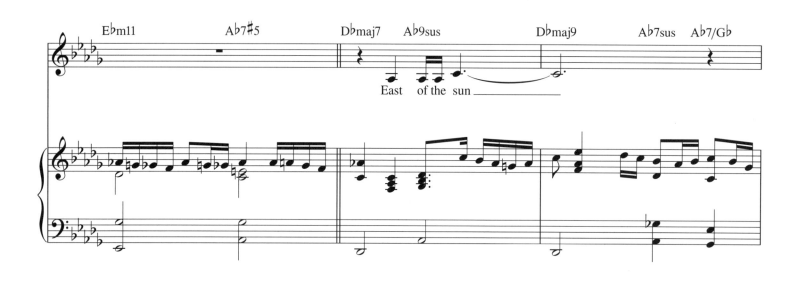
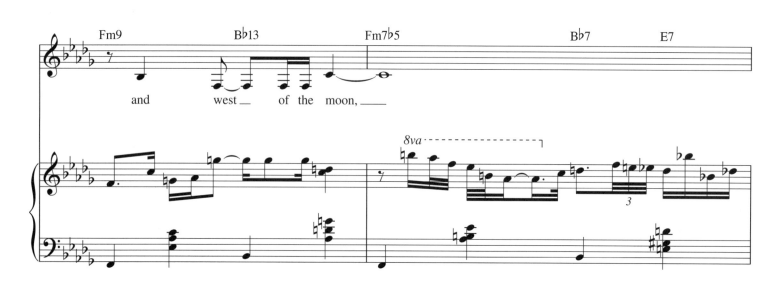

Copyright © 1934 by Chappell & Co.
Copyright Renewed
International Copyright Secured All Rights Reserved

LULLABY OF BIRDLAND

Words by GEORGE DAVID WEISS
Music by GEORGE SHEARING

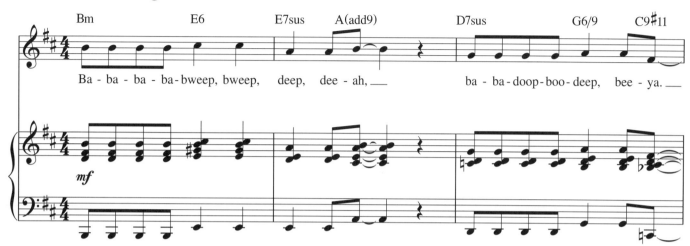

© 1952, 1954 (Renewed 1980, 1982) EMI LONGITUDE MUSIC
All Rights Reserved   International Copyright Secured   Used by Permission

IF YOU COULD SEE ME NOW

Music by TADD DAMERON
Lyric by CARL SIGMAN

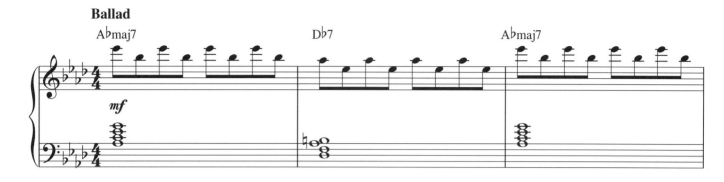
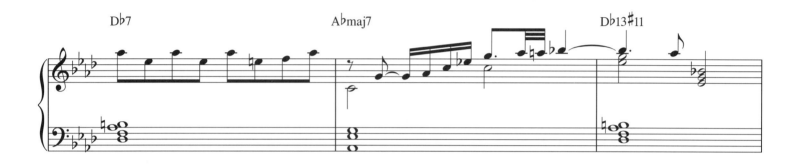
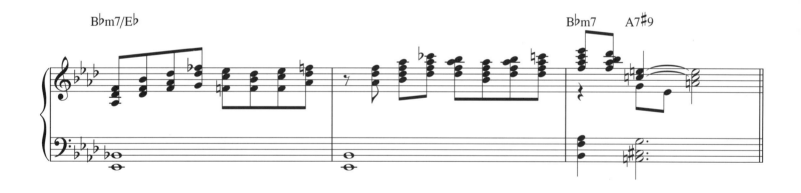

If you could see me now, you'd know how blue I've been.
If you could see me now, you'd find me being brave.

© 1946 (Renewed 1974) EMI Robbins Catalog Inc.
All Rights Controlled by EMI Robbins Catalog Inc. (Publishing) and WARNER BROS. PUBLICATIONS U.S. INC. (Print)
All Rights Reserved   Used by Permission

IT MIGHT AS WELL BE SPRING
from STATE FAIR

Lyrics by OSCAR HAMMERSTEIN II
Music by RICHARD RODGERS

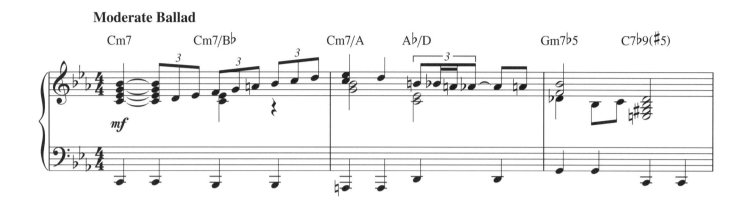

I'm as rest-less as a wil-low in a

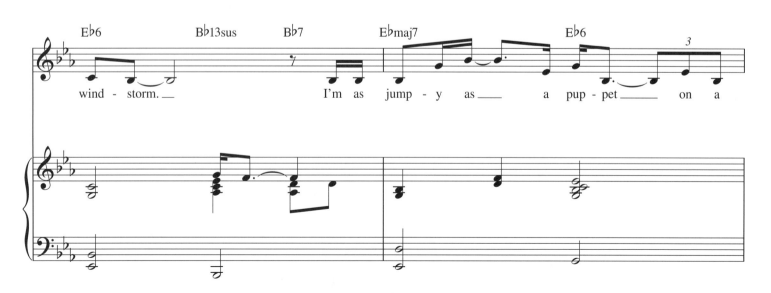

wind-storm. I'm as jump-y as a pup-pet on a

Copyright © 1945 by WILLIAMSON MUSIC
Copyright Renewed
International Copyright Secured All Rights Reserved

IT SHOULDN'T HAPPEN TO A DREAM
(How Could It Happen to a Dream)

By DUKE ELLINGTON, JOHNNY HODGES
and DON GEORGE

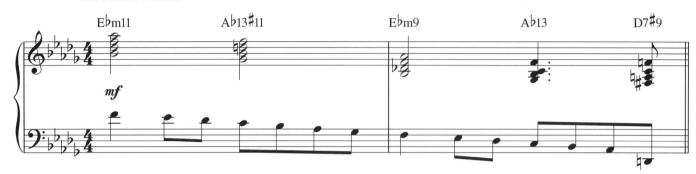

Copyright © 1946 (Renewed) by Music Sales Corporation (ASCAP) and Ricki Music Inc.
International Copyright Secured   All Rights Reserved

THE MAN I LOVE

Music and Lyrics by GEORGE GERSHWIN
and IRA GERSHWIN

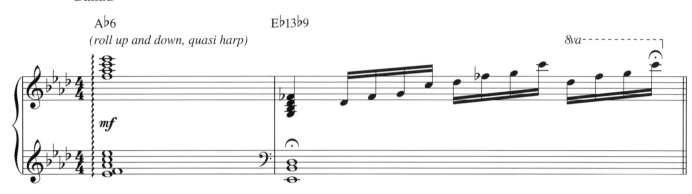

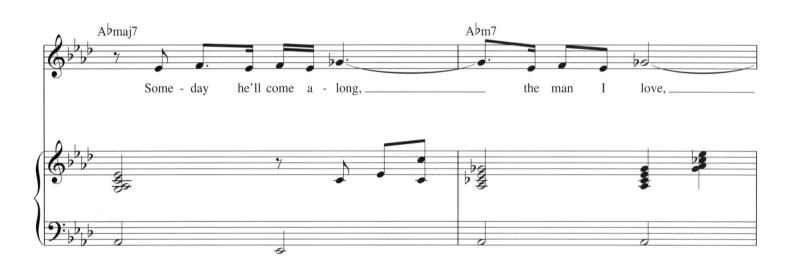

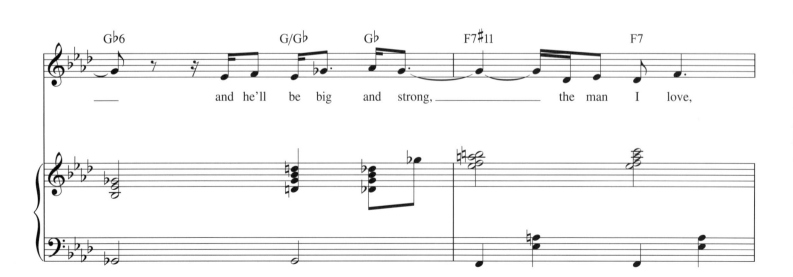

© 1924 WB MUSIC CORP. (Renewed)
All Rights Reserved Used by Permission

MISTY

Words by JOHNNY BURKE
Music by ERROLL GARNER

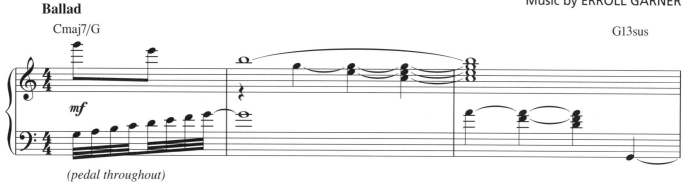

Copyright © 1955 by Octave Music Publishing Corp., Marke Music Publishing Co., Inc., Reganesque Music, Limerick Music and My Dad's Songs, Inc.
Copyright Renewed 1982
All Rights for Marke Music Publishing Co., Inc. Administered by BMG Songs, Inc.
All Rights for Reganesque Music, Limerick Music and My Dad's Songs, Inc. Administered by Spirit Two Music, Inc.
International Copyright Secured   All Rights Reserved

MY FUNNY VALENTINE
from BABES IN ARMS

Words by LORENZ HART
Music by RICHARD RODGERS

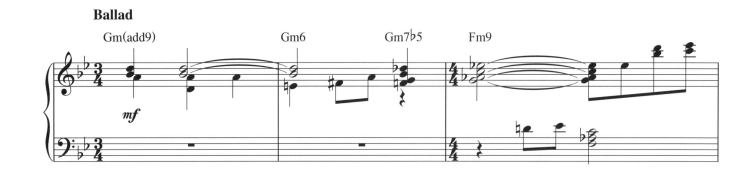

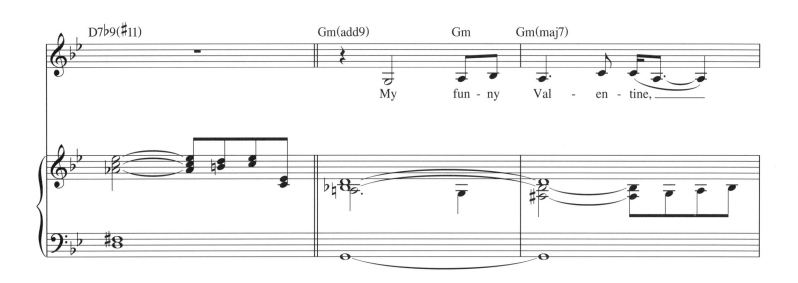

Copyright © 1937 (Renewed) by Chappell & Co.
Rights for the Extended Renewal Term in the U.S. Controlled by Williamson Music and WB Music Corp. o/b/o The Estate Of Lorenz Hart
International Copyright Secured   All Rights Reserved

MY SHIP
from the Musical Production LADY IN THE DARK

Words by IRA GERSHWIN
Music by KURT WEILL

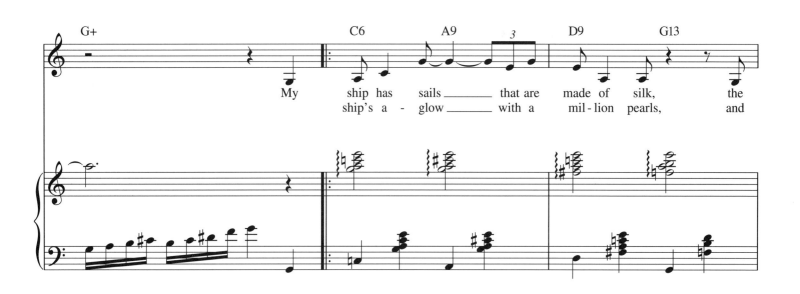

TRO - © Copyright 1941 (Renewed) Hampshire House Publishing Corp., New York and Chappell & Co., Los Angeles, CA
International Copyright Secured
All Rights Reserved Including Public Performance For Profit
Used by Permission

THE NEARNESS OF YOU
from the Paramount Picture ROMANCE IN THE DARK

Words by NED WASHINGTON
Music by HOAGY CARMICHAEL

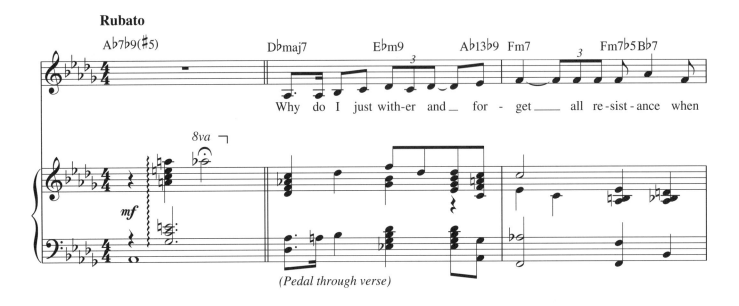

Copyright © 1937, 1940 (Renewed 1964, 1967) by Famous Music Corporation
International Copyright Secured   All Rights Reserved

A NIGHT IN TUNISIA

By JOHN "DIZZY" GILLESPIE
and FRANK PAPARELLI

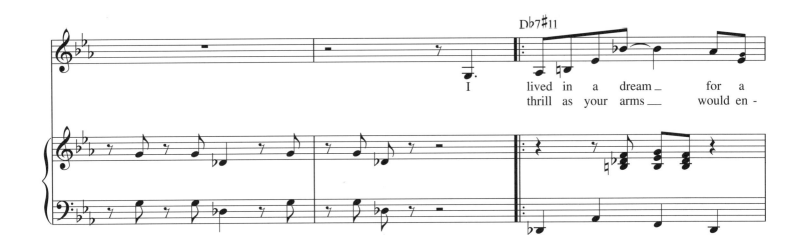

Copyright © 1944 UNIVERSAL - MCA MUSIC PUBLISHING, A Division of UNIVERSAL STUDIOS, INC.
Copyright Renewed
All Rights Reserved   Used by Permission

PERDIDO

Words by HARRY LENK and ERVIN DRAKE
Music by JUAN TIZOL

Moderately fast Swing

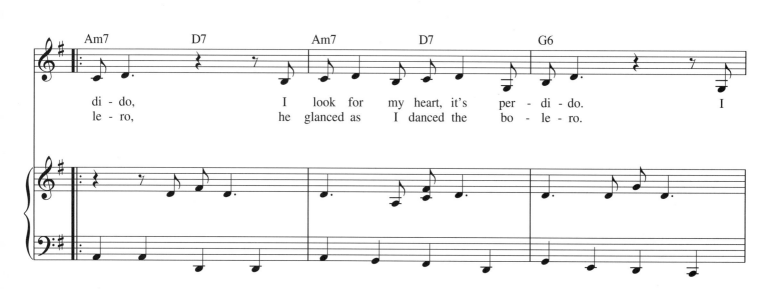

di - do,   I look for   my heart, it's   per - di - do.   I
le - ro,   he glanced as I danced the   bo - le - ro.

Copyright © 1942, 1944 (Renewed) by Tempo Music, Inc. and Music Sales Corporation (ASCAP)
All Rights Administered by Music Sales Corporation
International Copyright Secured   All Rights Reserved

AN OCCASIONAL MAN
from the Motion Picture THE GIRL RUSH

Words and Music by HUGH MARTIN
and RALPH BLANE

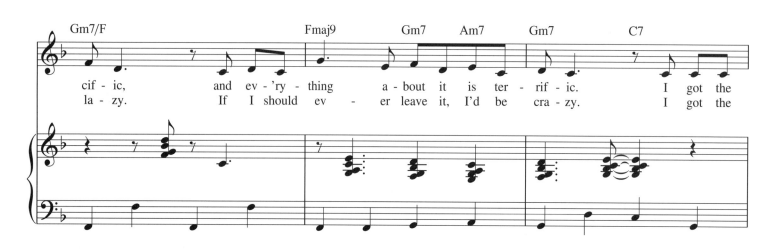

I got an is-land in the Pa-
is-land, it's ver-y

cif-ic, and ev-'ry-thing a-bout it is ter-rif-ic. I got the
la-zy. If I should ev-er leave it, I'd be cra-zy. I got the

© 1955 (Renewed) FRANK MUSIC CORP.
All Rights Reserved

SEND IN THE CLOWNS
from the Musical A LITTLE NIGHT MUSIC

Music and Lyrics by
STEPHEN SONDHEIM

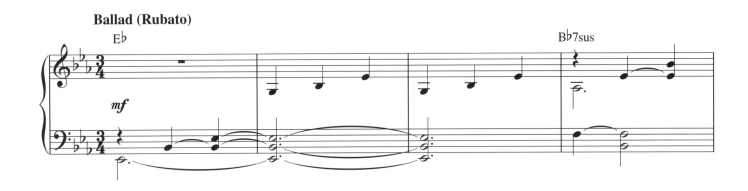
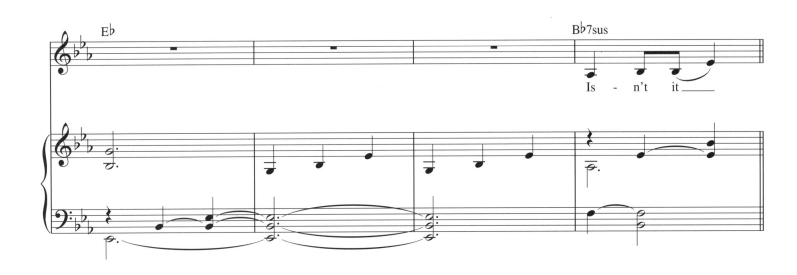
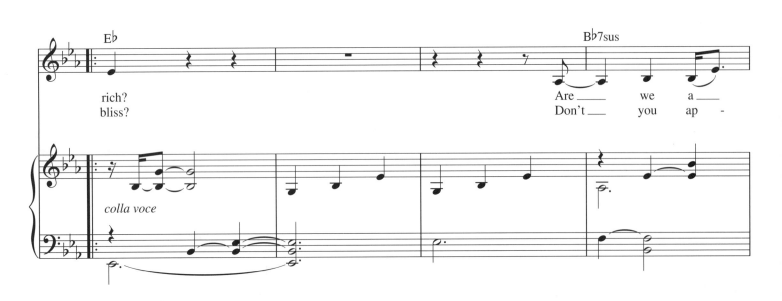

© 1973 RILTING MUSIC, INC. (Renewed)
All Rights Administered by WB MUSIC CORP.
All Rights Reserved   Used by Permission

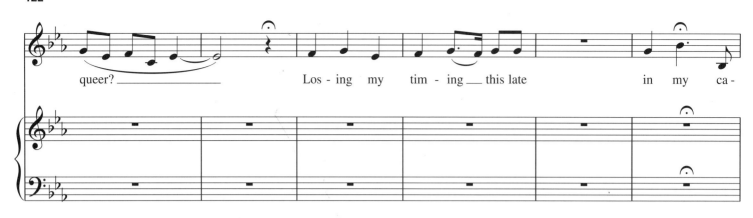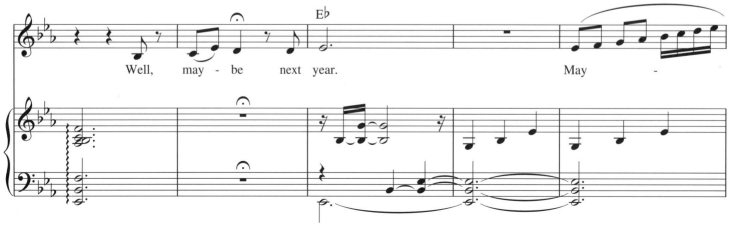

SEPTEMBER SONG
from the Musical Play KNICKERBOCKER HOLIDAY

Words by MAXWELL ANDERSON
Music by KURT WEILL

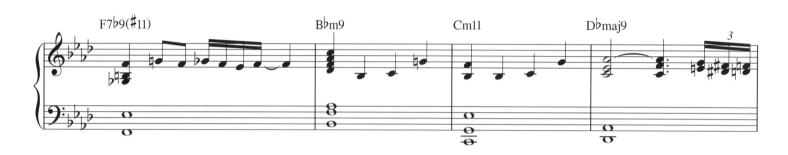

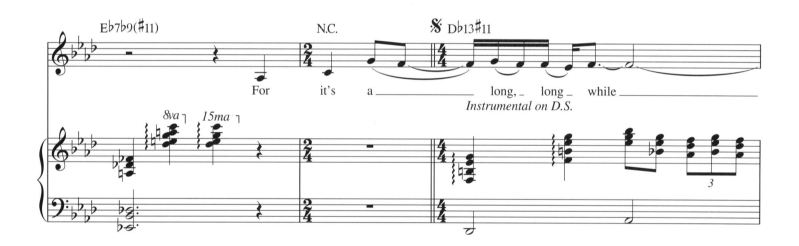

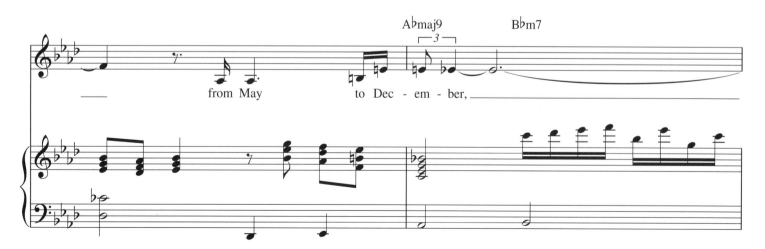

TRO - © Copyright 1938 (Renewed) Hampshire House Publishing Corp., New York and Chappell & Co., Los Angeles, CA
International Copyright Secured
All Rights Reserved Including Public Performance For Profit
Used by Permission

129

SPRING WILL BE A LITTLE LATE THIS YEAR
from the Motion Picture CHRISTMAS HOLIDAY

By FRANK LOESSER

Spring _____ will be a lit-tle late _____ this year, a lit-tle
spring _____ will be a lit-tle slow _____ to start, a lit-tle
Instrumental on D.S.

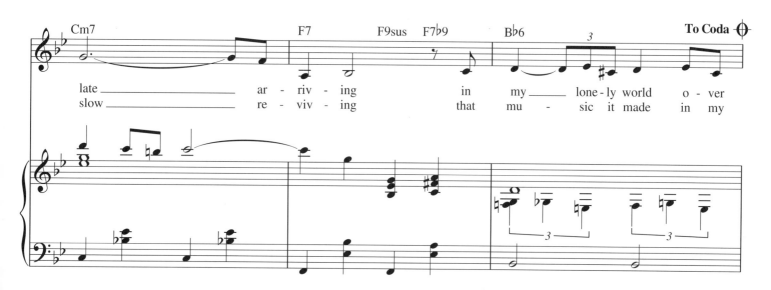

late _____ ar- riv- ing in my _____ lone-ly world o- ver
slow _____ re- viv- ing that mu- sic it made in my

© 1943 (Renewed) FRANK MUSIC CORP.
All Rights Reserved

TENDERLY
from TORCH SONG

Lyric by JACK LAWRENCE
Music by WALTER GROSS

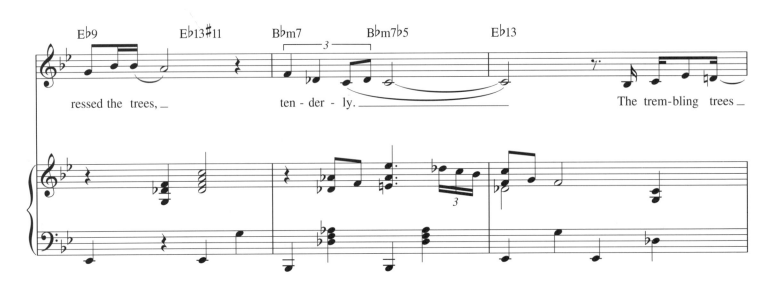

© 1946, 1947 EDWIN H. MORRIS & COMPANY, A Division of MPL Music Publishing, Inc.
Copyright Renewed, extended term of Copyright deriving from Jack Lawrence assigned and effective August 7, 2002 to RANGE ROAD MUSIC INC.
All Rights Reserved

Discography

After Hours – *The Divine Sarah Vaughan: Columbia Years 1949-53* (Columbia C2K-44165)

Black Coffee – *The Divine Sarah Vaughan: Columbia Years 1949-53* (Columbia C2K-44165)

Body and Soul – *The Complete Sarah Vaughan on Mercury Vol. 1: Great Jazz Years; 1954-1956* (Mercury 826320-2)

But Not for Me – *Jazz 'Round Midnight* (Verve 512379-2)

Cheek to Cheek – *The Complete Sarah Vaughan on Mercury Vol. 3: Great Show on Stage; 1954-1956* (Mercury 826333-2)

Cherokee (Indian Love Song) – *The Complete Sarah Vaughan on Mercury Vol. 1: Great Jazz Years; 1954-1956* (Mercury 826320-2)

Darn That Dream – *Jazz 'Round Midnight* (Verve 512379-2)

East of the Sun (And West of the Moon) – *The Divine Sarah Vaughan: Columbia Years 1949-53* (Columbia C2K-44165)

If You Could See Me Now – *Ken Burns JAZZ Series* (Verve 549088-2)

Isn't This a Lovely Day – *Sarah Vaughan & Billy Eckstine: The Irving Berlin Songbook* (EmArcy 822526-2)

It Might as Well Be Spring – *The Divine Sarah Vaughan: Columbia Years 1949-53* (Columbia C2K-44165)

It Shouldn't Happen to a Dream – *The Essential Sarah Vaughan* (Verve 512904-2)

Lullaby of Birdland – *The Complete Sarah Vaughan on Mercury Vol. 1: Great Jazz Years; 1954-1956* (Mercury 826320-2)

The Man I Love – *The Divine One* (ASV 5423)

Misty – *The Essential Sarah Vaughan* (Verve 512904-2)

My Funny Valentine – *The Complete Sarah Vaughan on Mercury Vol. 1: Great Jazz Years; 1954-1956* (Mercury 826320-2)

My Ship – *The Essential Sarah Vaughan* (Verve 512904-2)

The Nearness of You – *The Divine Sarah Vaughan: Columbia Years 1949-53* (Columbia C2K-44165)

A Night in Tunisia – *The Divine One* (ASV 5423)

An Occasional Man – *The Complete Sarah Vaughan on Mercury Vol. 1: Great Jazz Years; 1954-1956* (Mercury 826320-2)

Perdido – *Count Basie & Sarah Vaughan* (Roulette CDP7243)

Send in the Clowns – *Ken Burns JAZZ Series* (Verve 549088-2)

September Song – *The Complete Sarah Vaughan on Mercury Vol. 1: Great Jazz Years; 1954-1956* (Mercury 826320-2)

Spring Will Be a Little Late This Year – *The Divine Sarah Vaughan: Columbia Years 1949-53* (Columbia C2K-44165)

Tenderly – *The Complete Sarah Vaughan on Mercury Vol. 1: Great Jazz Years; 1954-1956* (Mercury 826320-2)